Shantika

The

Superhero

By

Clara Kennedy Witherspoon

Copyright © 2023 by – Clara Kennedy Witherspoon – All Rights Reserved.

It is not legal to reproduce, duplicate, or transmit any part of this document electronically or in print. Recording of this publication is strictly prohibited.

Dedication

"Shantika, The Superhero" is dedicated to every child who feels alone and scared and needs a peer hero who can empathize with their feelings and give them Hope.

Acknowledgment:

I want to acknowledge every parent and teacher who views a child as a whole person. And who strives to understand that a child needs a healthy parental attachment to develop into a healthy adult.

About the Author

Clara Kennedy Witherspoon was born in Monroe, NC, and educated in the Charlotte-Mecklenburg Schools System. She received a BA in Psychology from North Carolina Central University, a Master's degree in Christian Leadership from Liberty University, and the University of the Southwest in School Counseling and School Administration. She is the author of Who Me? A Superhero, playwright, and poet.

New Beginning

Shantika's eyes opened wide, remembering she had not finished her report due today. She looked at the clock beside her bed and thought, "I have plenty of time to finish my homework before Mom gets up; it is 5:30 AM." Shantika grabbed her bookbag and pulled out her partially completed Science report. She begins writing, finishes her science report, and returns it to her homework folder. "I will go ahead and get dressed for school," thought Shantika. While dressing, she reflected upon all she had learned and experienced over the past week. She recalled the Wisdom Tree's last words to her. Shantika smiled and finished dressing.

Once she was done dressing, she went into Will's room to get him up and ready for school. Encouraging Will to dress was always Shantika's hardest morning chore.

When Shantika's mom awakened at 6:00 AM, Shantika had completed all her chores, made up her bed, and was in the kitchen getting breakfast for Betty Ann, Will, and herself.

"Oh, you are up, said Shantika's mom." "Yes," said Shantika, and I have gotten Will dressed, and Betty-Ann is dressing now." I even made breakfast for us. Her mom replied, "Well, that was nice; what brought all that on?" Mom, you work hard and do your best to provide for us. I am so sorry that I have not helped out more. I promise that I am going to do better. Shantika's Mom looked at her, and tears rolled down her face. Shantika, I am sorry I have been so hard on you, but you are my only help. I know it is not your fault or that I should expect you to do so much because you are just a little girl.

I want us to sit down and talk when you get home from school today. Shantika looked at her mom and said, "I would like that."

At School

While walking down the hall towards her class, Shantika noticed, for the first time, that all teachers stood at the door entrance of their classrooms. Um, thought Shantika, "I never realized that all the teachers stood at their classroom doors." Shantika continued walking down the hall until she arrived at her class. Mrs. Rice smiles and says how are you this morning? "I am fine, said Shantika, and I am glad to be in school today." Mrs. Rice thought to herself, this child has changed. She reflected upon Shantika's behavior at the beginning of the school year and how disruptive she was during class.

Ms. Watson interrupted Mrs. Rice's thoughts. "Good morning, Mrs. Rice, said Ms. Watson." "You look like you are having a deep thought." Well, yes, I was thinking about one of my students. Do you see the student over to the left of my classroom?

Yes, said Ms. Watson. Her name is Shantika. Last year, she was in Ms. Taylor's class and always appeared angry. When I received my class roster this year, I could have dropped to my knees because Shantika was on my third-grade classroom roster. I asked Ms. Taylor about her, and she said, brace yourself; she will be the student who will challenge you all school year.

Ms. Watson replied, well, has she been difficult? Yes, said Mrs. Rice, all year until last week. Something has changed her behavior, but I do not know what, yet I am glad to see the changes in her. She can be a nice little girl. Ms. Watson replied, "Rice, have you ever sat down and talked with her?" "No, said Mrs. Rice; "she came into class with a look that conveyed to me, leave me alone, so that is what I do, leave her alone." Ms. Watson replied, well, that is a problem, Rice; many of our students come from homes where they must help with siblings or work to help provide for their entire family. Why don't you take the time to get to know her better? The bell rang, and all the teachers began to enter their classrooms and shut their doors. "Have a good day, Watson said Mrs. Rice." Ms. Watson waved bye and walked towards her classroom door.

"Good morning, students, said Mrs. Rice." I hope you had a wonderful weekend. Please take out your homework and put it in the homework bin on my desk. Next, we are going to do something special this morning. Alice, with the red hair, asked, what will we do differently? "It is important for us to take some time to get to know one another, said Mrs. Rice." We usually go right into our daily classwork. Today, I would like to have *Sharing Time,* where you can share what you did over the weekend or share about something that happened fun or made you sad. "We will do it every morning before beginning our morning work." Mrs. Rice asked the class if they would enjoy having *Sharing Time.* All the students in Mrs. Rice's class shouted yes, including Shantika. Well, go to the carpet and sit on your assigned carpet square.

When all the students were seated on their carpet square, Mrs. Rice said, who would like to go first? "I want to go first, said Melvin." "Okay, said Mrs. Rice, you will have 1 minute to share." I will ring the cowbell when your time is up. "Okay, said Melvin." My dad is in the army and came home yesterday; he has been gone for a year. My Mom, little sister, and I were so excited to see him. I missed him because I did not have anyone to teach me how to play baseball or to listen to me when I was sad. My dad is my best friend. I am so glad he is home! All the kids in the class clapped their hands for Melvin and said we are so happy your dad is home. "Thank you for sharing, Melvin, and I am delighted that your dad is home, said Mrs. Rice." Melvin, with a big grin, replied, thank you. Mrs. Rice asked, would anyone else like to share? Shantika raised her hand and said I would like to share. Shantika said a special friend helped me realize how hard my mom worked to care for my siblings and me. My Mom and I will have a girl talk when I get home from school today, and I am so happy about it.

Shantika finished her time of sharing and sat back down. Mrs. Rice pondered upon Shantika's remarks, yet she did not ask her any questions. "Thank you for sharing, Shantika," said Mrs. Rice. All the students clapped for Shantika. When Shantika's classmates clapped for her, she looked at them with a surprised look. Does anyone else want to share? If we do not have anyone else who wants to share, then class, please return to your desk and take out your math books.

During Lunch

"Sorry, Shantika, said Sarah." I didn't mean to step on your foot. Shantika stared at Sarah and slowly responded, "it's okay." Do you want to sit with me during lunch, asked Sarah. Wondering why Sarah was being nice to her, Shantika replied, yeah, I would like that. Sarah said we could sit with friends in different classrooms today because today is *Friend's Day*.

"I never participated in Friends' Day because I don't have any friends." Well, you do now, said Sarah.

Let's sit with Brandy and Sherrie. Hey Sarah, sit here by me, said Sherrie. "Okay, but can Shantika sit with us, too?" Sherrie looked up at Shantika and slowly nodded to indicate it was okay for Shantika to sit with them. Sherrie thought, Shantika is mean, and I don't like her. "Thank you, Sherrie, for letting Shantika sit with us, said Sarah." Sherrie did not respond to Sarah's statement but switched the conversation to her sleepover.

    Sherrie asked Sarah, are you coming to my sleepover? Yes, said Sarah, but I have to do my chores before I can come. Shantika turns and looks at Sarah and says, you must do chores too; I thought it was only me. Sherrie responds we all must do chores. I don't like to do them, but it helps my Mom.

    Okay, girls, says Mrs. Rice, your table is next; empty your lunch trays. Sherrie, I know I have not been nice to you, but thank you for allowing me to sit with you during lunch, said Shantika. Sherrie nodded okay and headed to the front of the cafeteria to empty her lunch tray.

Shantika and Sarah walked to the front of the cafeteria together. "Thank you, Sarah, for becoming my new friend," said Shantika. "I know I must show the rest of my classmates that I can be nice to them, and I will." Sarah smiled at Shantika and said, "I am glad you are my new friend."

Mrs. Rice called out to Sarah and Shantika to please get in line. Mrs. Rice walked her class to the hall where the girls' and boys' bathrooms were.

Outside on the Playground

Mrs. Rice said, students, you will have twenty minutes to play, and when you see me raise one hand and show five fingers, you know you will only have five minutes left to play. The next time you see my hand up, it is time to transition back into the line so we can return to class. All the children responded, okay, Mrs. Rice.

Most boys played tag, and the girls stood in little hurdles. Shantika looked around the playground to locate Sarah. Shantika sees Sarah sitting with Rebecca and Tray. Shantika walked over to where her new friend Sarah was sitting.

"Hi," said Shantika. Tray looked up with a surprised look on his face because Shantika never talked to anyone. Shantika asked Sarah, why are you looking so sad?

My Mom came to school, and I was called to the office. What did your mom want, asked Tray? She wanted to tell me my Aunt Phil would pick me up from school. Do you ride the bus home from school asked Shantika. No, normally, my mom picks me up. I feel something is wrong, said Sarah. I could see it all over my mom's face. Shantika asked, don't you think your mom would have told you if something was wrong? "I'm not sure; lately, my mom has not talked much to my sister or me said Sarah." Tray asked Sarah, "does your dad live with you?" "Yes, but he has been gone a lot. "It is because of his new job, said Sarah."

Shantika thought, "Sarah's parents are going to divorce." "How would I know that, thought Shantika?" She shakes her head and focuses her attention back on Sarah.

Mrs. Rice raises her hand, showing all five fingers, and five minutes later, she raises her hand again. "We better get in line, said Sarah." "Bye, Tray; I will see you tomorrow." Whose class is Tray in asked Shantika? Tray is in Ms. Watson's class, responded Sarah.

Shantika Talks with her Mom

"Come into the kitchen, Shantika, so we can talk while I cook dinner." "I will be right there, said Shantika." Shantika returns to the kitchen and stands near her mom.

Shantika, I hope you understand what I will try to explain. Let's sit at the kitchen table, said Shantika's Mom. Before you were born, your dad and I had a good marriage, even after you were born. I fell in love with your dad because he was a good listener. Shantika, you are like him in some ways because you are a good listener and think with your heart. Early in our marriage, we listened to one another, which was all so comforting.

Your dad and I had little material things, but we had one another. Shantika asked, well, what happened to you all? Money was so tight, and we would have to stretch it so far to cover bills, groceries, and the needs of our children. The money your dad made from his job needed to be more. I took a part-time job to help, but my job required me to work at night. Your dad cared for you during the evenings and would bathe each of you and put you to bed. I would be so tired when I got home from work. Our lives became a revolving door. Eventually, all we did was argue and fuss with one another. We fell out of love; I am not sure what happened. But I know it is wrong to transfer my anger to you.

Shantika began to cry. Shantika, "I am sorry that I transferred my pain to you." I will not get everything right, but I promise to be honest when overwhelmed. I know you won't always understand, but I will no longer transfer my frustrations to you. Wiping the tears from her eyes, Shantika said, okay, Mom, you should take a time-out

when you feel frustrated. Shantika's Mom smiled and said, you have a point, she reached out and hugged Shantika.

Sarah Finds Out What Is Going On With Her Parents

"Hey Sarah, wait, said Shantika." Are you on your way to the cafeteria for breakfast or to class? "No, I am not going to breakfast this morning," said Sarah." Oh said Shantika, are you okay? Sarah looked at Shantika with a sad look; my mom and dad are getting a divorce, said Sarah. I just found out this morning.

"Shantika dropped her head and said, I am sorry to hear that your parents are divorcing too." Why did you say too, asked Sarah. When I was in kindergarten, my parents divorced. How did that make you feel about them divorcing asked, Sarah. I did not like my mom for a long time because of how she treated me. Now that I understand why my parents separated, I love my Mom said Shantika. What changed your feelings about your mom asked Sarah. A lot of things changed, said Shantika.

"Oh, the bell just rang, said Sarah." We better get to class so we don't get into trouble. "I will see you on the playground, said Shantika." While walking to her class, Shantika asked herself, how did I know that Sarah's parents would divorce? The Wisdom Tree did not tell me I could see in the future. Shantika looked up, and Mrs. Rice was standing at the classroom door. "Good morning, said Mrs. Rice." "How is your day going?" Shantika was surprised Mrs. Rice was being so nice to her. Shantika responded, it's going well, and walked to her desk.

Once the second school bell rang, Mrs. Rice closed her classroom door. "Good morning, students; please place your homework in the bin on my desk, said Mrs. Rice." Once you have placed your homework in the bin, head to the carpet for *Sharing Time*. All the students hurried to sit on the rug. Christopher, a quiet student who never says anything, raised his hand to share first. Thank you, Christopher, for raising your hand first. What would you like to share, asked Mrs. Rice. "I am sad and wanted you to know, said Christopher." Mrs. Rice asked, why are you sad? My Mom told me not to tell anyone what was happening at home. I just wanted you to know that I am sad, said Christopher. "Well, okay, said Mrs. Rice, we can talk later."

Christopher nodded his head. Would anyone else like to share this morning? There was a sudden quiet inside the room, and no student responded. Finally, Leslie raised her hand. Mrs. Rice, I will be moving away to a new city, but I don't want to go, but my daddy got a new job. We would hate to lose you, Leslie; you are a part of our classroom family, said Mrs. Rice. Leslie responded, thank you. Does anyone else want to share this morning? If not, said Mrs. Rice, everyone can return to their desk and pull out their math book.

Classroom Independent Work Time

Christopher, please come up to my desk said Mrs. Rice. Christopher, do you want to talk with Ms. Johnson, the school counselor? She can help you feel better, said Mrs. Rice. "No, said Christopher, I don't want to see Ms. Johnson." My Mom told me not to talk about what was happening at our house. She said people would take my little sister and me away from her.

Shantika hears what Christopher is telling Mrs. Rice. However, she must be closer to Mrs. Rice's desk to hear their conversation. Shantika clearly hears every word Christopher is saying. Shantika realizes she can listen to sounds beyond her normal range and filter out distracting noises or conversations.

Mrs. Rice, can I return to my seat, asked Christopher. "Yes, but if you change your mind and would like to see Ms. Johnson, let me know."

Shantika watches Christopher return to his seat. He places his head on his desk. Shantika remembered when she felt blue. She would also place her head down on her desk.

Shantika closes her eyes, and suddenly, she is standing in Christopher's house in the middle of his living room. She looks around, sees a man waving his hand, and then begins screaming at a woman. Shantika' knows that she is invisible and cannot be seen. She continues to watch, and the man grabs the woman by her arm, and the woman starts to cry. The man screams louder and louder. Finally, Shantika opens her eyes and returns to her classroom. Mrs. Rice asked Shantika if something was wrong. "No," said Shantika. Shantika finds it hard to return to her work; she knows why Christopher is so upset. His mom is afraid of her boyfriend.

Shantika Learns More About Her Superpower

Lying in her bed, Shantika thinks about Christopher and his mom. And what he might be going through. She tries to figure out what to do or how she can help. Shantika knows she has been given a superpower and wonders how her powers could help Christopher.

Shantika looks for her special belt, finds it, and places it around her waist. As soon as she puts the belt around her waist, she is lifted into the air, spun around five times, and placed on her bedroom floor.

Shantika looks down at herself, wearing a brown suit with a yellow belt around her waist. An emblem in the middle of her belt is a picture of the Wisdom Tree. Shantika looks into the mirror, and she almost doesn't recognize herself. She begins twirling around in her room, careful not to awaken her mom or siblings.

Shantika began to test her powers, jumped from her bed, and nearly touched her ceiling. She placed the palm of her hand on her belt again and could hear her neighbors talking while in bed. Shantika recalled the Wisdom Tree, saying she could become invisible. Shantika was unsure how to become invisible, so she tried touching her belt to see if she would become invisible, but it did not work. She even tried jumping on one foot, but it did not work; she could still see herself in her bedroom mirror. Finally, she closed her eyes and opened them, and she could no longer see herself in the mirror. "I am a real superhero, thought Shantika." Yet, there is one more problem: how do I get around? " I don't know how to fly, said Shantika." Shantika stayed up most of the night practicing her new superhero skills.

Overslept

Mom called out, Shantika, are you up yet? Shantika jumped out of bed, Mom, I'm so sorry, I overslept! Shantika' Mom responded I have gotten everyone ready for school, and your breakfast is on the table. Shantika could not believe that her Mom had done all her morning chores and even fixed breakfast. "Thank you, Mom, said Shantika." Her mom looked around and said, no, thank you, Shantika! Shantika hurried into her bedroom and got dressed for school.

Sleepy in Class

Shantika could barely keep her eyes open during independent work time. Mrs. Rice calls out, "Reading group 2, go to the back table and bring your level two reading book." Shantika slowly got up from her desk and walked to the round table. "You look a little tired, Shantika said Mrs. Rice." Did you get enough sleep last night? "No, said Shantika." Well, do your best to try and stay awake said Mrs. Rice. Before we begin reading, students, let's cover our vocabulary words.

Shantika Tests Out Her Superpower

"Goodnight, Shantika, said her mom." "Goodnight, Mom." Shantika gets into bed and listens for her mom's bedroom door to close. The door shuts, and Shantika jumps out of bed. She looks underneath her bed and pulls out her Superpower belt.

She places it around her waist, twirls, her entire body raises to her bedroom ceiling, and gently returns to her bedroom floor. Shantika looked into her mirror, completely dressed in her Superhero suit. She smiles and walks straight through her bedroom walls onto the main street. She is wondering how she would find Christopher's house. As soon as the thought runs through her mind, she finds herself standing in Christopher's bedroom. Christopher is asleep, thinks Shantika; at least the house is quiet. Shantika starts to turn away and hears a door opening. She walks through the wall and enters Christopher's living area. Entering the house was a man with brown hair, and he was stumbling. Shantika watches him as he moves towards the couch, falls onto it, and goes straight to sleep. She decides to wait and see if he wakes up, but he never does, so Shantika leaves.

Christopher

"Good morning, Christopher, said Shantika." Are you on the way to your class or breakfast? "I am on my way to breakfast," said Christopher." Can I walk with you, asked Shantika. "Sure, said Christopher." Did you finish your math homework, asked Shantika. "Yes and no, said Christopher." See, my mom's boyfriend is kind of crazy, and if I do not go to bed early, he gets mad. So, I started my homework but did not finish it. Shantika asked, what do you mean, kind of crazy? Well, he sometimes hits my mom and me. But please do not tell anyone I told you this. I won't, said Shantika.

Someone Who Cares About You

Shantika waited until her mom and siblings were in bed, then dressed in her Superhero suit. Just in case her mom enters her bedroom, she places her pillow underneath her bed covers. Shantika turns and walks through her bedroom wall onto her neighborhood's streets. She looks at the sky and then closes her eyes while thinking about Christopher. Then, Shantika opens her eyes and is standing in the living room of Christopher's home. She enters Christopher's room and finds him fast asleep. Again, the front door opens, and Shantika enters the room to see who enters the house. It is Ron, Christopher's mom's boyfriend. Ron starts screaming Christopher's mom's name, Alice, get in here! Suddenly, Christopher wakes up and runs into the room. Ron screams at Christopher, get back in your room, boy! Crying, Christopher runs into his bedroom and gets into his closet.

Shantika looks at Ron, Alice's boyfriend, and suddenly, Ron is frozen. He cannot move or speak. Shantika walks into Christopher's room and becomes visible.

She opens the closet door where Christopher sits. Christopher is sobbing; Shantika places her hand gently upon Christopher's shoulder. He looks up at her and asks; Who are you? Shantika responds, "Someone Who Cares About You!" She sits in the closet next to Christopher. What are you feeling? "I fear Ron will hurt my mom, me, and my little sister." Oh No! said Christopher, "I need to check on my little sister." He jumped up, ran into the living room, and stopped.

What happened to Ron, asked Christopher. Shantika responds I froze him, and he cannot hurt anyone right now. I also made it so that your mom never heard him calling her. Your little sister is fast asleep.

Christopher, why do you think your mom stays with Ron? She does because he gives her money to buy groceries and helps her pay our rent. What do you want to happen in your family, asked Shantika. "I want us to leave this apartment and move away somewhere safe." Christopher, can you talk to anyone about your feelings, asked Shantika. I can speak with my school counselor, but my mom said not to talk about what is happening at home. Someone would take my sister and me away from her.

Christopher, your mom is not at fault, and no one will take you away from her as long as she is trying to keep you safe. When you get to school, see your school counselor tomorrow. She knows how to get your mom help, so she does not need to stay with Ron, said Shantika. For now, I will make Ron fall asleep on the sofa, and he will remain asleep until your mom, sister, and you have left the house. You can go back to bed and get a good night's sleep, but remember to see your school counselor tomorrow. "Okay, said Christopher, and thank you." Shantika turns and walks through the wall and back onto the streets.

Christopher Meets with Ms. Johnson

"Hey Christopher, wait, I will walk you to breakfast," said Shantika. Christopher turns around and looks straight at Shantika. I am not going to class or breakfast right now. "I need to see Ms. Johnson." "Oh, okay," said Shantika, I will see you later."

Christopher walks to Ms. Johnson's office and knocks on her door. "Good morning, Christopher, said Ms. Johnson."

Can I talk to you right now, said Christopher. Sure, let us go into my office, said Ms. Johnson. "Christopher, what is on your mind?" My Mom's boyfriend hurts my Mom and yells at my sister and me. I am afraid to go home because he may hurt us. Can you help us? "Yes, I can, said Ms. Johnson, but let me make a few phone calls to locate your family a safe place to live." Do you know your Mom's work phone number? "Yes," said Christopher." Ms. Johnson called Christopher's Mom and asked if she could come to the school. Go ahead and go to class, Christopher, said, Ms. Johnson. Everything will be fine.

"Thank you, Ms. Johnson, said Christopher."

Shantika's Mission Accomplished

Shantika walks into her classroom with a big smile. Mrs. Rice looks up and sees Shantika. "Good morning, Shantika." How are you doing? Shantika responds, "I am doing just fine!"

www.ingramcontent.com/pod-product-compliance
Lightning Source LLC
Chambersburg PA
CBHW051334110526
44591CB00026B/2999